Why Do Cats Do That?

Real Answers to the Curious Things Cats Do

By Kim Campbell Thornton

June Kikuchi, Editorial Director
Roger Sipe, Special Projects Editor
Karen Julian, Publishing Coordinator
Camille Garcia, Assistant Editor
Elizabeth Spurbeck, Assistant Editor
Jerome Callens, Art Director

Library of Congress Catalog Card Number: 96-80216
ISBN: 1-889540-01-3

BowTie Press®
A Division of BowTie, Inc.
3 Burroughs, Irvine, California 92618

Printed and bound in China.

15 14 13 12 11 10 09 1 2 3 4 5 6 7 8 9 10

Why Do Cats ...

A Present for Me?

Most of us have always acknowledged that cats are superior creatures; now we must accept that our cats know it, too. How else can we explain their need to feed us and help teach us to hunt by bringing us gifts of captured prey?

It must concern them that we are so inept at fending for ourselves. Cats, both wild and domesticated, have innate hunting skills, nurtured at an early age by the mother cat. She brings food back to her kittens, including live prey so they can practice their killing techniques. When our cats bring us prey, it could be that they are attempting to help us survive. Even spayed females exhibit this behavior. Maybe they are redirecting their maternal instincts to us, their surrogate kittens.

There may be another reason to explain this behavior. Wild cats instinctively bring their prey back to a safe area to eat, such as a tree or den. For a domestic cat, it may seem only natural to bring his catch back to his food dish because that's where he normally eats.

When your cat lines up live bugs on your pillow at 6 a.m. or proudly brings a mouse to your feet, accept the gift gratefully. Praise him for being such a good provider before discreetly disposing of the gift. ◆

FELINE FACT Garfield, the fat, lazy and utterly lovable cynic from creator Jim Davis, was launched June 19, 1978.

Chatter Cheese

If cats had a theme song for their daily hunting expeditions, it would no doubt be "Bite the Dust" by the Pussycat Dolls. That's exactly what's going through a cat's mind when he sees a potential meal outside the window. Imagine the feline frustration: "I know I could get that bird, I just know it, but here I am stuck behind this window." It's enough to make a cat gnash his teeth, which is exactly what he does.

When a cat spots prey, he displays his excitement by swishing his tail and chattering his teeth. However, the chatter isn't just frustration. The chomping action is the same killing bite he would use on prey. It is like he is carrying out the attack despite his inability to reach the target.

Cats make three general types of sounds — murmurs, yowls and strained, high-intensity sounds — and at least 16 distinct vocalizations. Chatter falls into the category of strained, high-intensity sounds, which may come from mom's training. She uses the sound to alert kittens to potential prey.

So the next time you see your cat chattering in the window, look out there with him. With your cat's expertise, maybe the two of you can take up birdwatching. ◆

KITTY CONDUCT Feed the birds and entertain your indoor cat. A bird feeder placed outside the window can provide your cat with some quality entertainment; don't worry, the birds quickly realize they are safe.

Plants Taste Good

Plant life is the last thing we would expect a carnivore to eat, yet eating greenery is one of the most common cat behaviors. They nibble delicately on plants and flowers, eating leaves and petals as if they were enjoying the most delicious salad. Then, they throw up on the expensive rug you found at the antique store.

Plant-eating cats concern many owners. Green stains on the carpet and poisonous plants make them worry. Some of the most common poisonous house and garden plants are dieffenbachia, English ivy and philodendron.

Eating plants may fulfill an instinctual need for greenery in the diet. Wild cats eat every part of their prey, including the grassy contents of their stomachs. Though theories have been proposed to explain this habit, it could be that grass provides fiber or vitamins and minerals not found in commercial cat food. Another possibility is that grass helps rid his system of hair swallowed during grooming. Whatever the reason, with the exception of harmful plants, eating greenery is a pretty harmless activity. As far as we can tell, cats do it because they like it. ◆

KITTY CONDUCT **To meet your cat's need for greenery, grow a box of oats or wheatgrass of her very own. This may prevent her from chewing on houseplants — which isn't very good for the plants — and it is a healthy alternative to eating grass outdoors.**

Cleanliness is Next to Godliness

Cats spend one-third or more of their waking hours grooming. The grooming ritual begins at birth when the mother cat cleans her babies. It is a way of establishing a powerful social and emotional bond, not only among cats themselves but also between cats and humans.

Although cats have a reputation for being independent, standoffish creatures, they have a clear social structure in which touch plays an important role. If you have ever seen cats meeting — usually at twilight on neutral territory — you may have observed them licking each other. Such social grooming is a way of reducing tension in a group situation: the cat's body relaxes, and his heart rate slows.

FELINE FACT Some cats groom excessively. Sometimes these cats are bored, perhaps because they receive little human or feline interaction. These cats suck obsessively at their fur, some even going so far that they mutilate themselves. A sick cat may groom less frequently or stop grooming altogether. Take this as a warning sign and get your cat to a veterinarian.

In addition to its obvious purpose — hygiene — and its social aspect, grooming helps cats cope with conflict. Have you ever seen your cat fall off the bed or caught him doing something forbidden? Usually, the cat's first response is to give himself a few nonchalant swipes with his tongue, as if he meant to fall off the bed. This type of grooming ritual is called "displacement behavior," and it helps the animal cope with confrontation, conflict or even embarrassment. Grooming indicates all is well.

Lastly, grooming benefits your cat physically. Whether with his rough tongue or your brush, grooming removes loose hair and parasites such as fleas, stimulates the skin, encourages the growth of new fur and helps regulate his body temperature through the cooling action of producing saliva.

To deepen your bond with your cat, set aside a specific time each week for grooming (daily for long-haired cats). Your cat will love the attention, and as a bonus he'll throw up fewer hair balls. ◆

Water You Doing?!

Few things are as amusing as a wet cat. He wears an expression of great disgust as he shakes the wetness from his fur. Then, he settles down for a long tongue bath to get his coat back in the proper condition, all the while sending indignant glares at the one who dared to bring him to such a pass.

Cats don't have the same protection from water that dogs have. Wet cats take longer to dry because they lack the oily coats and guard hairs that prevent dogs from getting soaked to the skin. But does this mean that all cats hate water?

Not at all. Many cats enjoy water and are known to fish and swim for enjoyment.

Throughout literature, many tales are told of cats who like to fish. (Indeed, the cat has his own built-in fishing pole: his tail.) Egyptian hieroglyphics depict cats hunting in marshes with their owners. Cats have been seen hooking trout and other fish out of streams with their paws. Cats have even been observed teaching other cats to fish.

So now we know. Cats don't necessarily mind getting wet, but it has to be on their own terms and for their own benefit. Needless to say, a bath does not fall into either of those categories for the average cat. After all, bathing is what a cat does best — with his own tongue, not with water and shampoo. ◆

KITTY CONDUCT If your cat needs a bath, gather your cat shampoo, towels and cotton balls and prepare the water first. The water should be warm, not hot. Put a rubber mat in the bottom of the sink or tub to prevent slipping. Now get your cat. Put cotton balls in your cat's ears to prevent water from running inside them, and place her in the water, holding her gently yet firmly. Wet her from the head down, being careful to keep water out of her eyes. Do not dunk your cat in water. Shampoo her (never use shampoo made for people or dogs). Next, rinse your cat thoroughly and towel-dry her until she is damp. Keep the cat in a warm, draft-free area until she is completely dry.

Eyes See You

A cat's unusually large eyes are perhaps his most striking features, and never more so than at night, when they seem to glow in the dark with an almost supernatural light. The cat is a nocturnal prowler, and his powerful sense of vision is what makes him so successful. But how exactly do his eyes work? Can a cat really see in the dark, using only those glowing eyes? Well, not quite. Here's how it works.

The feline eye structure includes the **cornea**, which is the clear, curved part of the eyeball in front of the pupil; the **iris**, which gives the eye its color; the **lens**, located behind the iris; the **retina**, consisting of a network of light-sensitive cells; and the ***tapetum lucidum***, a Latin term that translates as "bright carpet." The cornea, lens and retina work in much the same way as a camera. The cornea acts as the viewfinder, taking in light and transmitting it to the lens. The lens bends the light rays, focusing them to form an image on the retina.

Where does the *tapetum lucidum* come in? It is what allows the cat to take in extra light in dim situations. Lining most of the back of the retina, the *tapetum lucidum* acts as a mirror, reflecting light that was not absorbed the first time it passed through the retina. The result is the glow, called eye shine, that you see when light strikes your cat's eyes in a dark room. A cat can't see any better than you when it's completely dark, but when some light is available, the *tapetum lucidum* allows the cat to make better use of the light.

Why do some cats' eyes glow red while others glow green? Not because of any demonic influence. The color of the light reflected back from the *tapetum lucidum* relates to the cat's eye color. Green or yellow eyes tend to reflect greenish light; blue eyes, tend to reflect reddish light. ◆

Upright and Ready

Cats have a legendary ability to land on their feet after a fall. But is it true that cats always land on their feet? That depends, interestingly enough, on the height from which they fall.

When cats fall, they rely on two organs to bring them down safely: their eyes, which help cats position themselves correctly; and their *vestibular apparatus*, located in the inner ear, which controls balance and orientation. An automatic sequence of motions goes into play when a cat topples. First, the cat rights his head. Then, he rotates the front half of his body 180 degrees.

FELINE FACT Are you impressed by your cat's incredible sense of balance? Cats have an organ — the ***vestibular apparatus*** — within each ear that works with the eyes to give your cat her impressive balancing ability.

Once the front legs are facing down, the cat rotates the rear half of his body and flattens out to spread the area of impact. The tail acts as a counterbalance. As the cat hits the ground, he arches his back to help cushion the impact.

Why does the height from which a cat falls make a difference? Falling from a great height allows more time for this sequence of motion to take place. Cats who fall from shorter distances are often hurt more severely because they don't have time to react properly.

Why do cats fall from high places? Mainly, it's because their depth perception isn't very good. Apparently, they do not realize that they're about to jump eight stories instead of eight feet.

Just because a feline survives a long-distance fall doesn't mean he can't be injured. Broken legs are a common result of falls, so kids don't try this at home. Your cat will thank you. ◆

KITTY CONDUCT **Do you sometimes catch your cat chasing a bit of dust or a flying insect? Chances are your frisky cat would enjoy a fishing pole–type teaser toy with an object you can float through the air to tease her.**

Sounds Like Nirvana

Cats love crinkly sounds. Crumple a plastic or paper bag and watch your cat's ears snap to attention. Like his tail, your cat's ears are expressive, twitching and turning to catch each sound. The same thing happens when a cat hears a squeaky toy or any high-pitched sound.

Is there a reason that these types of noises elicit greater interest than others? Of course! Our mighty feline hunters rely almost as heavily on their ears as they do on their eyes. Crinkly or squeaky sounds are similar to the high-frequency noises made by small animals such as mice, birds and crickets; thus, they immediately draw a cat's attention and often trigger the prey response, such as pouncing and stalking.

A cat's ears are always on alert. Even when he's sleeping, you may notice a slight twitching in response to sounds that might indicate danger. When it comes to hearing, cats have it in the bag. ◆

FELINE FACT **Cats' ears are incredibly sensitive. They are able to detect sounds as high as 65 kilohertz, an ability that may be even greater than that of the dog and a cat's hearing is far better than a human. The highly mobile *pinna*, or ear flap, permits the cat to move her ears in the direction of a sound, allowing her to determine the source of a sound with a high degree of accuracy.**

Knead to Know Basis

The American South is known for its colorful colloquialisms and none more so than "The cat is making biscuits," which describes cats "kneading" with their paws. (The saying is especially descriptive for cats with white paws, which look as if they have been dipped in flour.) The reflexive action of pushing the paws in and out on a soft surface harkens back to a time of pure pleasure: when a cat is snuggled up to his mother, safe and warm, kneading as he drinks her milk. A kneading cat is the epitome of contentment.

The kneading behavior develops at birth when the newborn pushes forward in an attempt to find his mother's nipple and presses with his paws to stimulate the flow of milk. In most cases, it continues throughout the cat's life, appearing during times of relaxation and contentment. We can suppose that the cat who kneads is remembering kittenhood.

Like all mammals, cats are extremely sensitive and responsive to touch. For them, touch is an important means of communication. Pleasing touch, like petting, can stimulate kneading behaviors. A female in heat kneads in anticipation of mating. Not surprisingly, the cat's forepaws are unusually sensitive (which could explain why so many cats dislike having their paws handled or rubbed).

FELINE FACT Laser pointers are great toys to use to get your cat active. The small, red, laser dot shining on the floors or walls is enticing for most cats and can keep your cat on the chase for a long time.

For humans, few things are as pleasurable as the massage given by a cat's soft paws. Now, if only we could teach our cats to keep those paws extended and to work on sore shoulders and backs. ◆

Prey Play

Kittens learn to kill and eat prey by practicing on live victims provided by their mother. A cat's habit of "playing" with their prey before administering the kill is related to the high level of arousal brought about by the thrill of the hunt. Because cats are attracted by motion, prey that tries to escape may motivate a cat to continue stalking and pouncing until he tires of the game or becomes stimulated enough to deliver the killing bite. When the prey is finally dead, the cat may be so excited that he continues to play.

But not all cats carry through the hunting behavior to its logical conclusion. Hunting and killing are learned abilities. A kitten who doesn't learn these skills from his mother will have no idea how to kill a mouse or bird. Instead, attracted by the sound and movement, he will play with the animal as he would with a toy. Cats who do learn hunting skills may need the stimulation of stalking and pouncing to trigger the killing instinct. Prey that is inactive may not elicit the fatal bite.

Even if your pet is not a Mom-trained mouser, when you see your kitten or cat pouncing on a ball or chasing his tail, you are seeing prey behaviors in action. ◆

KITTY CONDUCT When it's time to replace your cat's worn-out scratching post, take it slow. Bring home the new post, place it beside the old one and give your cat up to a week to get used to the new item. Then, feel free to remove the old post from your home.

A Purr-fect Explanation

People love the sound of a cat's purr, but the soothing sound is still not very well understood. You probably think a purring cat is a happy cat, but this explanation doesn't cover all the bases. Cats purr not only when they are happy but also when they are stressed, for instance at the veterinarian's office. Think of the purr as the cat's equivalent of our smile, indicating that no hostile intent is meant.

How cats purr has long been a mystery. In a Breton folktale, cats are said to have developed the purr after spinning 10,000 skeins of linen thread to help a princess break an enchantment. It's easy to understand how a cat's purr could be compared to the whir of a spinning wheel.

Today, however, the mystery has been solved. The sound a cat makes is caused by vibrating muscles surrounding the larynx. Researchers have also discovered where the purr originates: in the brain. Stimulation of a specific area in the cat's brain causes cats to begin purring.

The purr is one of the first sounds newborn kittens make, as they snuggle up to their mother for milk and warmth. As they mature, their purr becomes more complex. While young cats tend to purr in monotone, adults are capable of reaching two or three notes and sometimes as many as five. Purring can go on for hours without a break, even while a cat is eating or sleeping. In fact, it has been suggested purring is a form of a snore. Purring cats often drool as well. The combination of salivation, purring and paw kneading in an adult may indicate a temporary regression to feeding time in kittenhood. ◆

FELINE FACT It was once believed that the big cats did not purr, but experts have discovered that wild members of the genus Felis, which includes bobcats, cougars and lynxes, purr like domestic cats. Members of the genus Panthera — lions, tigers, leopards, panthers and jaguars — purr, but only while exhaling, unlike domestic cats, who purr while inhaling and exhaling. The difference may be a matter of throat formation.

Going Belly Up

Flop. That's the greeting many cat owners receive when they return home. Snowball runs to the top of the stairs, meows a hello, then falls over in a heap, as if all his bones suddenly melted. He rolls on his back and extends his paws in welcome.

Surely this must be one of the greatest of all cat gifts. When you think about it, a cat who rolls over in greeting is indicating complete trust and faith in the person or animal to whom he is rolling. When a predator such as the cat exposes his belly, he is saying, "I am completely comfortable and content around you. I know that you would never hurt me." (Not that this means you can get away with actually rubbing his belly. Often, that requires an even higher level of trust and comfort.)

Cats roll over for a number of other reasons. Sometimes it means they want to play. For a cat-style wrestling match, put a couple of thick athletic socks over your arm and rub your cat's belly. He can rabbit-kick to his heart's content without leaving your arm a bloody mess. (Cats are smart. They quickly learn this is allowed only when the socks are on.) Or, pull out the kitty fishing pole and dangle it above him. Watch him roll as he tries to grab the end of the line. When this occurs, your cat may be displaying a form of defensive behavior, even as he plays. A quick roll allows a cat to grasp and claw his adversary.

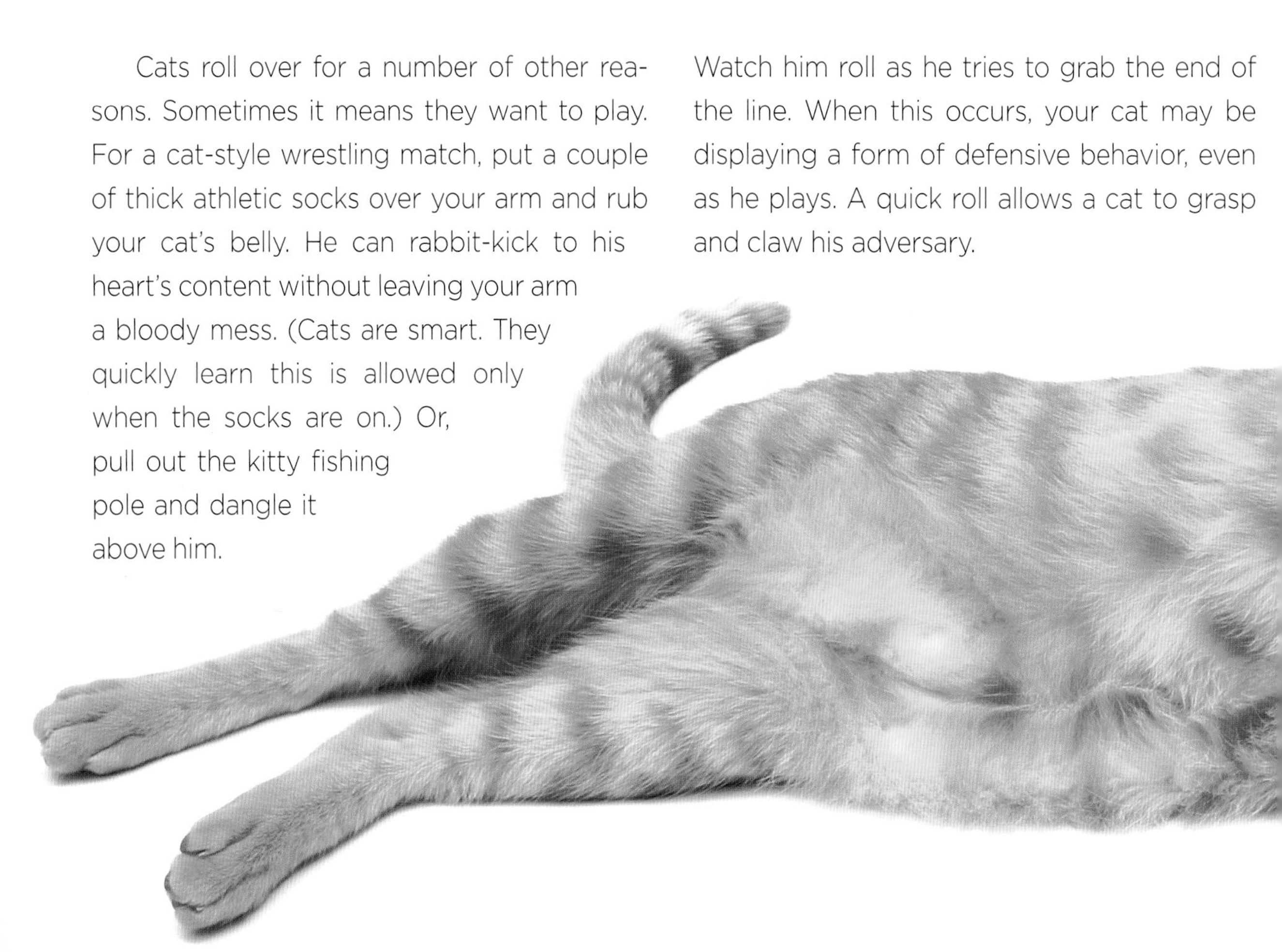

Rolling is also a form of foreplay. During courtship, the female rolls suggestively, enticing the male with her sinuous movements. You may see this behavior in a cat playing with catnip. So the next time your cat flops over when you come home, you'll know that you've received the greatest compliment a cat can give: his trust. ◆

FELINE FACT Does your cat seem to purr very loud at certain times of the day? Experts say that a loud purr invites close contact or attention, so indulge your cat and appreciate her desire to spend quality time with you.

Rub You the Right Way

Our cats twine sinuously around our legs, rubbing insistently with their heads. Is this action a demand for food or a friendly greeting? Most of us tend to assume the former, knowing how meaningful meals are to our cats; but, what we are actually experiencing is a combined feline greeting and claim of ownership.

Cats have scent glands distributed over their bodies: the perioral glands on the lips and chin, the temporal glands on each side of the forehead and the caudal glands along the tail. Although the scent emitted by these glands (unlike the scent of cat urine) is undetectable by humans, it serves an important role in feline and feline/human social rituals. One cat approaching another often raises his tail in greeting. If the second cat also raises his tail, the two will then rub against each other.

Cats also greet their people in the same manner, butting heads with them or rubbing up against their hands or legs. Not only is this a friendly gesture, it also allows the cat to indicate to all and sundry felines that this person is his. In fact, cats who mark excessively in this way may be nervous or unsure of themselves. So the next time your cat gives you a nice head butt or swirls his tail around your legs, thank him for the compliment and reassure him that you will always be his devoted and loving owner. ◆

KITTY CONDUCT

Brushing or combing your cat removes loose hair, reduces shedding and spreads skin oils, all while helping you bond with your pet.

Furniture Fervor

Does your pet have cat scratch fever? No, not the disease — the desire to claw only the finest furniture, wallpaper and draperies! Well, you're not alone. Scratching is an innate feline behavior, and it is something all cat owners must learn to deal with.

Cats scratch for several reasons. First, scratching keeps their claws in shape. You schedule a weekly manicure; your cat schedules a scratching session with the sofa. Not only does scratching sharpen the claws and remove the old outer husk of the nail, it just feels good. Think how great it feels when the manicurist massages your hands and arms. Your cat probably gets a similar pleasurable feeling from scratching.

Scratching also serves as a territorial marker. Cats may scratch in preferred sleeping spots or any other place where they spend a lot of time. Doorways and windowsills often get scratched, especially when an indoor cat spots an intruder outdoors. He scratches in a vain attempt to let the other cat know that this is his territory.

Scent is another aspect of territorial scratching. The sebaceous glands in a cat's paws leave an odor at the area scratched, another way the cat can stake his claim.

To make sure your cat scratches only in approved areas, think on his level. Cats like to scratch sturdy, vertical objects such as trees. That's why they often choose a chair or sofa as a substitute. Cats like to stretch tall when they claw. Provide your cat with a scratching post at least three feet high. This allows your cat to stretch out to his full length, tail included. Cats like to scratch things that are rough. Choose or make a post that is covered in material such as sisal or burlap. Avoid carpet because your cat will not be able to tell the difference between the off-limits carpet on the floor and the carpet on the post. Or attach the carpet to the post so that only the rough underside is showing. Some cats like scratching bare wood or logs covered with bark. Provide them with their own small "tree" in the house — a stable log placed so the cat can stand on it and scratch.

Place the scratching post in a convenient area. If you hide it, your cat may not be attracted to it. A corner of the living room or bedroom is a good spot. Also, beware of moving the post. Cats may protest if you change what they consider the natural order of things. ◆

KITTY CONDUCT **To teach your cat to use the post, run your fingernails up and down it. The sound and motion will attract your cat. Sprinkling catnip on and around the post is another good way to heighten a cat's interest as well as giving the cat a treat whenever she scratches in the appropriate place. Always praise your cat when she uses the post and discourage her with a water squirter when she attempts to use anything else.**

It's Naptime

Somewhere

Sleep, eat, sleep, play, eat, sleep. Sleep a little more. Dream about fishsticks, mouse-burgers, the dog sleeping outside. Eat. Sleep some more. This feline schedule is no exaggeration. Cats sleep up to 18 hours a day, much more than most other mammals. Such a restful lifestyle is not limited to domesticated cats. Wild cats have been described as living a life of inactivity punctuated by searches for food. It's clear that housecats see no reason to alter this way of life.

It's not known why cats sleep so much. Perhaps it is related to their solitary nature. Apart from lions, which live in groups called prides, cats are the Daniel Day-Lewis of the animal world: They want to be alone most of the time. And because they don't read or watch television, they do the next best thing:

sleep. You might say that cats are the original couch potatoes.

How much sleep a cat gets depends on his stage of life and lifestyle. Kittens and old cats sleep the most. A warm, well-fed, contented cat will sleep just about any time. Cats who are confined, such as those in catteries or boarding kennels, while away the hours with catnaps. Cats normally sleep in brief spurts, but cats whose owners work full-time may sleep all day, saving their waking hours for morning and evening, when they can socialize with their people.

Do our cats dream? Yes, they do, and they are as active in a dream state as they are when they're awake, twitching, swishing their tails and making noise. What are they dreaming about? Well, unless they start talking in their sleep we'll never know, but my guess is that they're finally catching that elusive, mocking sparrow out in the back yard. Or maybe they're just reliving their latest meal. ◆

FELINE FACT **Despite the fact that cats are such experienced sleepers, they are as good as alarm clocks — and sometimes worse. If you don't want your cat waking you up every day at 4 a.m. to feed him, never respond to his pleas. Not even once. Cats learn very quickly, and once they realize they can get you out of bed by yowling or meowing, you're history. Teach your cat to let sleeping people lie.**

C-mail

Inquiring minds want to know. Whose territory is this? How long ago was he here? Is he ready to mate? How old is he? Like a distant early warning system, a cat's urine spray contains pheromones — chemical substances that stimulate behavioral responses — that inform other felines of the cat's age, sex, sexual receptivity and how long ago he passed by. This allows a passing cat to determine whether a rival is in the area and whether to continue on his way or take another route. You might call it a sort of time-sharing arrangement. When the scent from the first cat fades, it's safe for another cat to pass through.

Scent marking also acts as a sign of ownership or an invitation. When your cat sidles

KITTY CONDUCT **If your cat starts spraying in the house, examine your lifestyle for changes. Cats are creatures of habit, and change can cause them to feel the need to state their presence. You can try to prevent spraying by placing aluminum foil or plastic over the area sprayed so that the urine makes a noise or splashes back on the cat; by neutralizing the odor and then feeding the cat in that area (cats don't like to soil their dining rooms); or simply keep the cat away from the area. Squirt your cat with water when you see her move into position.**

up to a vertical object such as a tree or light pole — or your new sofa — backs up, positions his quivering tail, and emits a pungent spray of urine, he is sending a clear message to intruders: this is mine! Unlike a dog, a cat who comes across the scent mark of another cat will not spray over it. Instead, he makes his mark in a nearby area. Female cats in heat spray to indicate their availability. Their urine contains hormones, the scent of which attracts male cats from miles around.

Indoor cats can be just as territorial as their outdoor brethren. It's not uncommon for indoor cats to mark their territory by spraying, especially if there are too many cats in the home or if a new cat is brought into the household. Cats may also claim ownership of their people by marking areas that smell like their owners.

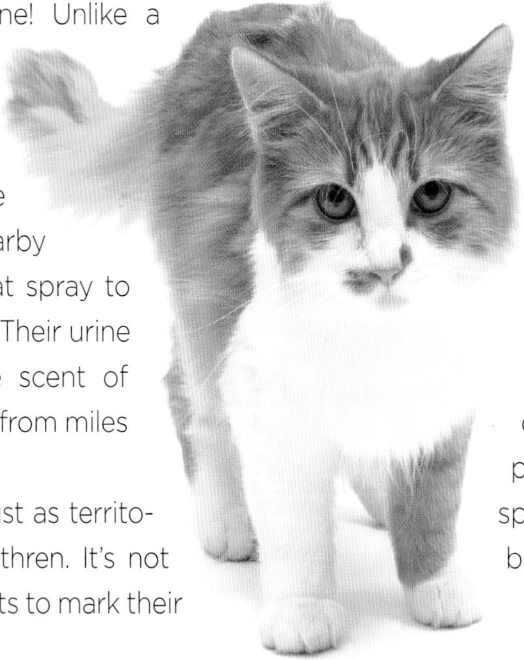

Unneutered males start spraying at sexual maturity, usually 6 to 8 months of age. To nip spraying in the bud, neuter male cats before 6 months of age. A neutered cat can still spray if the urge is strong enough, but the odor of his urine is not as powerful. Female cats who are spayed have no need to spray, but they may still go through the motions. ◆

Nom Nom Nom

Like a baby sucking on a pacifier, your cat may suck on blankets, afghans or clothing, especially those made of wool. Common in Siamese and Burmese cats (although it is seen in other breeds and mixes), this abnormal nursing behavior is thought to have a number of causes, from a lack of fiber in the diet to stress. One theory suggests that it occurs in kittens weaned too early; thus, they never naturally lost the urge to suckle. Perhaps the scent of lanolin in the wool resembles that of the mother cat's nipple. In the case of Siamese and Burmese cats, wool-sucking may be an inherited behavior.

A cat who merely sucks gently on items made of wool should probably be left alone. While it's annoying to find small wet spots on your favorite sweater, mildly obsessive sucking isn't really something that should cause serious concern. After all, many cats are neurotic to some degree, and punishing him could make the situation worse. The real problem begins when sucking gets destructive. Your cat may wear holes in wool items or even swallow pieces of wool.

A buildup of wool in the stomach can cause serious intestinal obstruction, which often requires surgery. ◆

KITTY CONDUCT How can you wean your cat from wool sucking? That depends on why the cat is sucking. Start by offering foods that are high in fiber such as dry cat food, wheatgrass or oats. If fiber doesn't help, substitute a toy each time you find your cat sucking on something inappropriate. Praise her when she sucks on the toy instead.

Sometimes, stress is the culprit. You may notice that wool-sucking occurs at certain times. Try to break the pattern by playing with or grooming your cat to replace the sucking behavior. If all else fails, try prevention. Spray your cat's favorite items with something distasteful such as Bitter Apple spray. Put woolen items out of reach. A wool-sucking cat is one way to make sure that clothes stay picked up.

Tail Talk

In addition to their sophisticated vocal skills, cats speak to us in another way: with their tails. To the person fluent in felinese, the movement of a cat's tail can speak volumes, expressing such emotions as happiness, excitement or anger.

Can you interpret your cat's tail talk? It's a pretty easy language to learn. You can judge your cat's emotional state by the speed and position of his tail. A happy or relaxed cat waves his tail slowly. All's right with this cat's world. A tail held high serves as a greeting. Kittens approach their mothers with tails up, an approach that is perhaps reminiscent of when Mom licked the anogenital area to stimulate elimination. They carry over this body language when greeting humans or other animals.

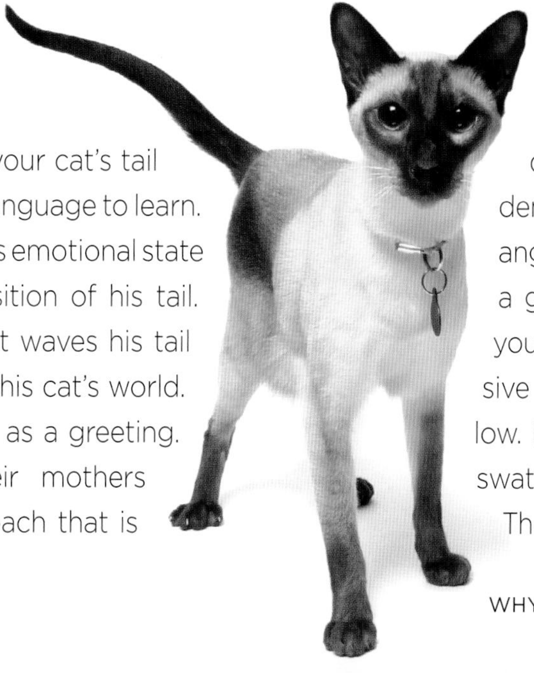

The tail is even more expressive when the cat is angry, aggressive or on the defense. A fast-moving tail denotes annoyance verging on anger. This cat is not happy. It's a good idea to put him down if you're holding him. An aggressive cat crouches with his tail held low. Don't be surprised to see him swat at or spring on his adversary. The cat under fire uses his tail to

FELINE FACT Meowing comes in a variety of pitches, rhythms, volumes, tones and pronunciations. This part of feline communication covers a wide range of meanings and purposes, from greeting, making demands or warning against anger.

fool his enemy. By arching the tail and fluffing his fur, the cat makes himself look bigger and scarier. Sometimes, this posture is enough to make a dog turn tail and run.

Just about every feline mood can be told by the tail. Why is the tail such a versatile means of communication? The answer lies in his skeletal construction. The feline tail has as many as 28 vertebrae, making it very mobile. The next time you pull your cat's tail, don't be surprised when he uses it to express his opinion of your rude behavior. ◆

Litter Box Lessons

The great thing about getting a cat is that he arrives fully assembled, with no training necessary — except on the part of the owner. Unlike a puppy, who must be painstakingly house-trained, a kitten is already programmed to use a litter box. All you have to do is show him where to go.

How did cats come to acquire this neat habit? It's an inborn matter of self-preservation. In the wild, cats bury their feces to hide their presence from predators or territory rivals. Our domestic house cats continue the habit, which is one of the things that make them such clean companions. This urge to hide his presence is so strong that even if a cat eliminates outside his box, he will still go through the motions of digging and covering.

Although the litter box habit is deeply ingrained, there are several instances in which a cat may stop using his box. This can lead to a messy situation, but by doing a little detective work, you can soon set your cat back on the proper path.

The first thing to consider is whether your cat is ill. Take your feline to the veterinarian for a complete checkup to rule out any physical problems. If he gets a clean bill of health, make like Ace Ventura and consider elementary factors such as cleanliness, type of litter or household changes. With his sensitive nose, any cat would be turned off by a box that isn't scooped frequently. Cleaning the box of its contents on a daily basis may solve the problem.

Some cats are picky about the type of litter used. Scent and texture are very important to them. If you're using a scented litter, try unscented. If you're using granular litter, consider replacing it with soft, sand-like clumping litter. Such a simple change can make all the difference to our fastidious felines.

If all else fails, try to think of any recent changes that may have stressed your cat. Cats are creatures of habit. A new baby, a new dog or cat or even a change in household routine can send sensitive cats around the bend. Moving the litter box can be especially problematic. If possible, make changes gradually so your cat will have time to adjust, and, give him extra attention to combat his insecurity. ◆

KITTY CONDUCT **Completely clean the inside your cat's litter box weekly. Dump all the litter, use a mild detergent and rinse thoroughly. Once dry, provide fresh litter. Also: Give your cat some privacy. Place litter boxes in quiet, semi-private areas, away from foot traffic and her food dishes.**

A Final Meow

One common answer to most questions that begin with "Why do Cats" is: because they are cats. Cats might be domesticated but many fanciers argue that it was the cat who domesticated humans (not the other way around!).

So the next time your cat is doing something that you think is strange, think about how many things you do that drive him nuts, like pet the dog, take away his favorite wool sweater or throw away his gift; he caught that for you, remember?

And though we would like to make our cats happy and fulfilled every moment of their lives, we can't be 100 percent correct all of the time. Even Albert Einstein failed at this. His housecat tended to become depressed when it rained, and when the weather was rainy, Einstein was known to say to the cat, "I know what's wrong, dear fellow, but I don't know how to turn it off." ◆